50 cents

Psychedelics and the College Student

SUPPLEMENTED EDITION WITH A NEW SECTION ON Amphetamines and Barbiturates

Student Committee on Mental Health

Princeton University

PRINCETON UNIVERSITY PRESS

Supplemented Edition, 1969

Published by Princeton University Press
Princeton, New Jersey 08540

Copyright © 1967 by
Princeton University Student Committee on Mental Health
All rights reserved.
L.C. Card: 67-30454

No part of this book may be reproduced
in any form or by any means
without written permission from the
Princeton University Student Committee on Mental Health,
Princeton, New Jersey 08540.

Introduction: Psychedelics

As recently as 15 years ago, drugs like marijuana and LSD were the concern of few and were used by even fewer. During the last few years, however, the use of psychedelic drugs has spread throughout society, especially among college students. And quite recently, the national press has picked up the drug question and has disseminated more information. But the two original sources for those on the campus who are actively interested in drugs, in one way or another, have been bull sessions and scientific journals. The former is apt to mislead; the latter, to be too obscure.

And just a few years ago, there were those who could prefer to ignore the question entirely and could get by with it. But now, that number is decreasing rapidly. Psychedelic drugs are now becoming so widely used that most—especially those concerned with the colleges—cannot help but be interested in the issue.

This study attempts to give a clear, two-sided picture of psychedelic use on campus. Any one section must be considered in the context of every other.

This study is not, by any means, a professional view of psychedelics, although professionals were consulted, and although the committee members did research into their particular units. The report is the work of an interested group of Princeton students, under the auspices of the Princeton Class of 1968, although Princeton itself is not the only campus under consideration.

It is intended to be an overview, nothing more. But above all, it is a statement of concern, concern which will—hopefully—lead to more interest and study of the problems on all college campuses.

Committee

Members

Percy Ballantine, II
James J. Britt
Steven H. Buck
Robert T. Burdsall
Harry Harding, Jr.
Mark E. Lackritz
Kim J. Masters, Chairman
Willner Park, Graphic Designer
Dermod F. Quinn
Daniel Sanders
J. Selby Smith
S. Linn Williams, General Editor

Consultants

Willard Dalrymple, M.D.
Director, University Health Services

James B. Laughlin
Assistant Dean of Students

William S. MacNaughton
Director, Counseling Services

Contents

1	Introduction: Psychedelics
4	Glossary
7	Legal Aspects of Drug Use
8	Medical Aspects of Drug Use
11	Social Aspects of Drug Use
16	The Psychedelic 'Experience'
16	A Successful Trip
17	An Unsuccessful Trip
19	Counsel and Information
20	Conclusions
21	Bibliography: Psychedelics
25	Introduction: Amphetamines / Barbiturates
25	Legal Aspects
26	Medical Aspects
26	Amphetamines
27	Barbiturates
28	Sociological Aspects
30	Counsel and Information
30	Bibliography: Amphetamines / Barbiturates

Glossary

Addiction
: a state of chronic intoxication produced by repeated consumption of a drug; its characteristics include (1) an overpowering desire or need to continue taking the drug and to obtain it by any means, (2) a tendency to increase the dose, (3) a psychological and physical dependence on the effects of the drug so that illness results from cessation of intake, and (4) a detrimental effect on the individual.

Amphetamines
: stimulant drugs such as dexedrine, methedrine, and benzedrine; often known as "goof balls."

Barbiturates
: depressant drugs which can be addicting.

DMT
: dimethyltryptamine, a non-addicting psychedelic drug; normal dose is 50 to 60 milligrams and the effects last about half an hour.

Habituation
: a psychological dependence on a drug with a strong desire to continue taking the drug for the sense of improved well-being or satisfaction which it engenders, as distinct from the physical dependence of addiction.

Hashish
: a concentrated form of marijuana's active element, the resin obtained from the flowers of the cannabis plant.

Heroin
: an opiate and narcotic; an alkaloid from the poppy plant.

LSD
: lysergic acid diethylamide; by weight, the most potent psychedelic drug; normal dose is 100 to 300 micrograms and the effects last from 8 to 10 hours; non-addicting.

Marijuana	a non-addicting drug obtained from the flowering tops of the cannabis or hemp plant.
Mescaline	the pure, non-addicting alkaloid derived from peyote; normal dose is 300 to 800 milligrams and the effects last from 8 to 10 hours.
Narcotics	a group of addicting drugs; the most common are the opiates: heroin and opium.
Opiate	any medicine containing or derived from opium.
Peyote	the unconcentrated preparation from the cactus plant, Anhelonium williamsii, non-addicting.
Psilocybin	a non-addicting drug derived from a type of mushroom; normal dose is 20 to 60 milligrams and effects last 5 to 6 hours.
Psychedelics	a group of non-addicting drugs which alter perception and consciousness; with experience one can decrease the dosage and get the same effects; the more common types are marijuana, hashish, LSD, DMT, peyote, and mescaline.
Set	the personal variables of a psychedelic experience such as personality, expectations, values, anxieties, desires, and one's degree of self-understanding.
Setting	the external conditions of a psychedelic experience such as the surrounding or location, the people present, the size of the group, the time of day, the degree of privacy, and the experience of the guide.
STP	4 methyl, 2, 5 dimethoxy alpha-methyl phenethylamine; a psychedelic chemical related to mescaline and amphetamine, said to be extremely mind-distorting.

Legal Aspects of Drug Use

It is beyond the scope of this report to explain the complex of state and federal law. Recent legislation adds to this complexity. The committee consulted several lawyers who observed that a precise codification and explanation of such laws would be difficult due to the absence of definitive case law.

The use of most psychedelic drugs is, above all, illegal. This present relationship of drugs to society—both on-campus and off-campus—should be a starting point. It is not for this report to debate that legality, merely to observe it. And the future problems—in employment and in admission to some graduate schools, for example—of a police record for 'drug use' are significant, regardless of the type of drug.

States vary in their classification of psychedelic drugs and in the penalties prescribed. LSD in some states is classified as a 'dangerous drug,' with mild or moderate penalties for its abuse. In at least one state it is classified as a narcotic. Some states have no state law pertaining to LSD. Federal law and many state laws classify marijuana and hashish as narcotics.

As an example of state law, in New Jersey most offenses with marijuana are high misdemeanors, comparable to felonies in most states. Any person who possesses, sells, has under his control, persuades others to use, dispenses, administers, gives away, compounds, mixes, manufactures, or prepares hashish or marijuana is guilty of a high misdemeanor. First offenses are punishable by a fine of no more than $2,000 and imprisonment at hard labor for two to fifteen years. Any person who commits a similar offense with other psychedelic drugs, such as LSD, is a disorderly person, the least serious classification of offense under New Jersey law. Any person apprehended under the influence of marijuana is also classified as a disorderly person. The penalty for disorderly person offenses is a fine of no more than $1,000 and/or a term of imprisonment up to one year.

Medical Aspects of Drug Use

The effects on the human body and mind of psychedelic drugs such as marijuana vary widely and are by no means entirely known. Although after study, this committee feels that the bulk of medical evidence indicates that the medically deleterious effects on individual and public health from alcohol are currently as great as marijuana, this does not excuse neglect of the effects of the illegal drugs.

At this point, it is necessary to make a medical distinction among certain kinds of drugs. The reader is referred to the GLOSSARY at the beginning of this report (pages 4 and 5) for those definitions.

The distinctions among drugs are important, for some drugs—fortunately—have only limited popularity with those college students who experiment with drugs, and thus, can be dismissed quickly for the purposes of this study. The opiate narcotics, especially heroin, are dangerous for at least three reasons:

1. They addict physiologically, so that withdrawal causes illness, sometimes death.
2. They are readily subject to overdosage. Recent studies have concluded that about 1% of heroin addicts in New York City die each year merely from overdosage.
3. Other physical and mental damage results from their prolonged use.

Both the 'sedatives' (especially barbiturates) and the 'stimulants' (mainly the amphetamines) have their significant dangers, particularly an addiction to barbiturates, which is very difficult to break. The risks and physiological harms are not unlike those of the opiate narcotics.

The third group is that of the psychedelics. It is this group which has been increasingly popular on college campuses, and it is this group we shall examine.

The most potent of these drugs is LSD (lysergic acid diethylamide).* LSD distorts the user's perception of the physical and psychological environment, often severely. Shapes, colors, sounds, tastes, touches, and emotional feelings are much different. Although careful selection of subjects and careful control of the environment and psychological conditions of the LSD 'trip' do give some protection against the possibility of harmful effects, it is now impossible to control those effects entirely.

Nausea, occasionally prolonged, palpitation, and sweating are among the physical changes produced. A handful of deaths have occurred, either from suicide or from misinterpretation of the environment, and some hundreds of prolonged psychoses are well-documented. No one knows precisely how LSD will affect another, or even himself.

A variety of other psychedelic drugs are available through underground channels: peyote and psilocybin from natural sources, and a growing list of synthetic products, of which the most common at the moment seems to be DMT (dimethyltryptamine). None is nearly as potent as LSD per unit of weight, but in other respects their effects approach those of LSD.

Pharmacologically, the mildest of the psychedelics is marijuana, although—as the LEGAL ASPECTS section points out—it is classified as a narcotic under the Harrison Narcotics Act. Marijuana can cause nausea and disturbances of the nervous system if used in high enough dosage. It can also cause distortion of perceptions of the environment, although not as intensely as LSD. Relating the medical element to the social element, such distortions might precipitate a traffic accident, for example, if the user drove while under the influence of marijuana. A recent report by the Harvard Health Services found examples of severe mental disturbances lasting a few hours among marijuana users.

The most potent form of marijuana is a concentrate

* There have been recent reports of a new drug, STP, which is said to be more mind-distorting than LSD

called hashish, usually originating abroad. The effects of hashish approach more nearly the severity of LSD than the ordinary forms of marijuana.

In addition, both marijuana and the other agents are often 'cut' (diluted) with unknown fillers, some of which may be toxic and some of which have contained poisonous heavy metals. The purity of the drugs obtained from illegal channels is sometimes undependable. Drug researchers advise that mixing drugs can be extremely harmful, especially mixing amphetamines with other drugs.

While the psychedelics do not cause the physical dependence that the opiates do, they can result in habituation. (Please see the GLOSSARY for medical evaluation of these terms.) Their long-term effect on behavior and social adjustment can be significant. General physical and mental deterioration in chronic hashish-users is reported from other cultures, although this is difficult to evaluate for the United States. The long-term effects of chronic LSD usage are essentially unknown. Recent scientific evidence from animal experiments suggests that LSD may produce chromosomal breaks and deformities in offspring.

Some experimental centers in the United States are presently working with psychedelics in the psychiatric treatment of alcoholism, homosexuality, criminal sociopathology, and neuroses.

Whether users of marijuana or any psychedelic are led to the use of other drugs has been the subject of continuing debate and research. Although nothing in the physical effects of the drugs seems to produce such a phenomenon, the sociological and psychological concomitants of drug usage apparently may create temptation to other drug use. Moreover, those with poor control over their impulses and those whose emotional lives are otherwise deficient are frequently among those using drugs of all sorts.

Social Aspects of Drug Use

Any honest discussion of the social aspects of the use of psychedelics on college campuses must admit before it begins that the conclusions it derives are, at best, generalized statements based on partial evidence. But the generalized statements can often be useful, for there are certain elements which are fairly representative of the over-all picture of student use of psychedelic drugs. The percentage participating in the different types of drug activity vary from campus to campus, but some of the basic patterns hold true for most of the universities which have been studied by various researchers.

There have been many recent attempts to categorize the type of student who is experimenting with psychedelic drugs. But types of drug experimenters have changed considerably in the United States in a relatively short period of time. Drugs have moved from the province of criminals to the intellectuals and the middle-class and, somewhere in between these, the college students.

With the growth of drug use, the students experimenting with psychedelics include athletes and scholars, science majors and art majors, rich and poor, devout and agnostic, socially popular and socially rejected. In each of these groups, something in the psychedelic experience may draw some for different personal needs and interests. No generalization can be made saying that all drug-takers fit a certain mold.

There are essentially two broad groups of students interested in actually using drugs, groups which the committee will call "social" and "insight" for lack of better words.

To the "social" groups, marijuana is smoked for essentially the same reasons that other groups use alcohol: escape from temporary pressures and worries to reach a mental condition at which it is easier to have uninhibited social enjoyment and intellectual relaxation. They feel that marijuana gives a more sensually pleasurable "high" feeling, that it does not have hang-over effects (although smoke may cause nausea).

The groups which use marijuana on campus vary in their involvement in student activities and in their general integration into the university life. The student in these groups for such social reasons are drawn from all sectors of the student body. And the groups themselves are usually rather solid social units, forming a base of acceptance and comradeship. Of course, students may also become members of off-campus groups.

But the possibility of student "informers" to police remains a threat which might undermine a group's social unity.

This social approach to marijuana emphasizes the role of the small group: the way others look at it and the way it looks at itself. The newcomer associates with the group's social image, whether that image is labelled as "bearded" or "cool." In addition, marijuana smoking is at least as communal as drinking alcohol to such groups; often, in fact, the marijuana is placed in one pipe, then passed around. This group activity is a source of acceptance, reducing the newcomer's uncertainty regarding marijuana.

There is another type of user which the committee has grouped under the "social" label: those members of the student body who are not integrated into the more normal social life of the university or college. Such isolated groups are merely one stage away from the earlier "social" groups: they are usually in varying stages of revolt against what they consider "the system," more often than other student groups.

At times, such persons use marijuana or alcohol for the same reasons as the previous "social" groups: temporary escape and social facilitation. At other times, however, they use marijuana for a retreat from situations which the individuals refuse to face. There are cases of such use which "helped get the students through the trying stages of college life." But such reliance can lead to situations which can be seriously damaging when the individual is thrust into society's demands and realities, immediately upon graduation.

Two other elements of importance pertaining essentially to marijuana.

Some argue that the purchase of marijuana involves the individual with the most undesirable parts of society. Others reply that this charge does not apply to college campuses. Students get marijuana from their friends. Students are rarely exposed first-hand to underworld elements. As applied to society in general, the defenders have argued that sellers are "undesirable" only because they sell drugs.

Drug users often claim a desire to rise above "middle-class mediocrity" in refusing to be bound by laws which they consider unjust and inconsistent. Why should marijuana be illegal when alcohol is not, they contend. Moreover, they continue, why should marijuana be considered more censurable legally than such drugs as LSD? "Declaration of personal independence" and "removal from the crowd" are often cited as reasons for drug use.

Opponents of this view contend that the users are merely conforming to non-conformity—especially with the growing use of drugs among college groups and among groups labelled as "intellectual" within the colleges themselves. They further contend that such an argument is given largely by those who take drugs only to prove their "liberal" leanings.

So much for the "social" users.

There is another group that has been developing most recently, a group which we have termed the "insight" group. These students too may smoke marijuana for reasons such as depression, insecurity, or rebellion. But their purpose is often more specifically "to gain psychological insight." Whether the "insight" is true or merely imagined is still the subject of medical and psychological examination, and perhaps it depends on individual cases

At any rate, it is this group which is most ready to try the more powerful psychedelics, such as LSD and DMT Information on the motives for trying these drugs is not yet very substantial, even less substantial is information concerning the ensuing experiences

The outcome of a psychedelic experience induced through ingestion of LSD or a similar chemical is influenced by several factors The first is setting, or the environmental atmosphere in which the drug is taken For experimental, optimal conditions experimenters try to make the setting hospitable, familiar, and without any possible sudden alterations The individuals present are usually limited to one or two close friends, who are familiar with the effects of the psychedelic drugs, in which an experienced person takes the drug with an inexperienced one, and another experienced guide "stays down" to control the trips This "guide" has the responsibility of providing the person taking LSD with an adequate tie with reality Because an individual "high" on LSD is influenced by suggestions, limited control of the type of experience—pleasant or unpleasant—is possible in most instances under such ideal, experimental conditions

Under the ideal experimental conditions many individuals taking LSD—in the proper setting and set—have been able to pass through possible traumatic parts of an LSD experience without suffering permanent psychological harm But the potential danger of unpleasant moments and —much more important—of permanent psychological damage, must be realized as a possible outcome even in such optimal circumstances Without those circumstances, the chances of mishap are considerably increased

Those who use the drugs argue that—given the proper setting, guide, and personality preparation—many have what they consider to be worthwhile experiences through

LSD: religious, aesthetic, intellectual, or purely sensual. In any case, they say the "trip" is often an insight into the taker's own personality: it magnifies that personality and lets the taker know more about himself.

Others disagree. They contend: either that LSD and such psychedelics alter and distort the basic personality structure, not magnify and illuminate it; or that psychedelics show an imagined personality, not a real one.

But there is some area of agreement. A poor "guide," a hostile setting, or an unbalanced personality can cause the individual to experience a temporary horror show—or possibly a permanent mental problem. Abnormal psychological states—such as schizophrenia, for example—often remain hidden to the person who has them. In such cases, LSD can—and has—caused permanent damage.

Right now, the debate over LSD is more emotional than factual or academic. Many of the facts simply are not there. Research is now being done, dealing with controls for the psychedelic experience. In time, those who might like to try LSD might be able to take a psychedelic chemical with some confidence in what will follow in his mind. But at the moment, any student experimenting with such drugs as LSD is taking a risk.

Among the "insight" group of users, many search for personal meditative, religious, or mystic experiences. Others of the same group use LSD and other such psychedelics to try and study the operations and possibilities of their minds. Once again, some say that this use has led to a greater control over the mental processes. Others contend that it can lead to loss of control, often leaving a permanent negative mark on the individual personality.

The use of LSD can also apparently alter the personality itself. Some have psychological problems: research being done with childhood schizophrenia works along this line. Others find a "new personality" dramatically different and frightening. Any student opting to try a psychedelic drug should consider this possibility. We must emphasize, however, that all preparations still leave the outcome uncertain.

The Psychedelic 'Experience'

Each individual's psychedelic experience is unique. Therefore the evaluation of any such experience is difficult. It may be useful in trying to understand the use of drugs to look at two aspects of that experience. Both accounts are fictional, written by members of the committee. But they are based on actual opinions and facts—as far as they can be determined—concerning LSD "trips."

A Successful Trip

"My sixth LSD experience started as I took 400 micrograms of LSD and waited thirty minutes for it to take effect. The first stage of the 'trip' was one of pure sensory ecstasy. LSD magnified enormously my capacity for aesthetic experience of music, art, architecture, and nature. Space and time changed. Sometimes it was stretched out as my mind worked faster and music sounded slow enough to be savored note by note. At other times, it varied between normal speed and a dead halt as my attention switched from the action around me to my own thoughts. My perception of distance and magnitude kept changing. Occasionally I could consciously control the variation. Walls seemed to bend as if made of a flexible material. I also experienced synaesthesia, an integration of my senses; I could see music emerge from the speakers and drift toward me in three dimensions and in color.

"The second stage was one of recollection and self-analysis. My ability to remember, and practically relive, many long-forgotten incidents was amazing. My self-understanding was greatly increased; it was something like going through several years of psychoanalysis in a few hours. I recognized that some of my values and attitudes result from particular incidents in the past which were traumatic. I learned a great deal about myself and this knowledge has helped me with the questions which I am now facing regarding my future.

"On this 'trip' I went beyond the second stage for the first time. The third stage is a non-verbal stage of symbolic images. Historical, mythical, and archetypal images filled my mind. Most of them involved characters and situations which said something about mankind and the meaning of life.

"The highest stage was close to a mystical experience. I find it difficult to express what little I can remember of this experience, but I felt that all my thoughts, emotions, sensations, and memories were fused into total understanding of myself and my place in the world."

An Unsuccessful Trip

"It was not my first trip that ended in chaos, it was my third. On my first two, my experiences were apparently conventional. There were gaudy lights, the grotesquely real new ways of looking at people, the rapid experiencing of sights, sounds, and feelings. My friends told me that this was expanded consciousness, and so I believed them. Afterwards, I did seem to be able to have new insights on my friends and family, at least after talking with my friends, and I was willing to overlook the very frightening moments of anxiety early in the trips through which my guide helped me.

"But it was my third, as I say, which was disastrous. Why, I cannot say. The dose was supposed to be the same (but you can't be sure, of course, unless you're a chemist and have made it yourself). The room was the same, and the guide was there with me. I anticipated greater ecstasy.

"But it was early in the trip that I noted that his face was more distorted than usual—strange, I never noticed how ugly he could be. And why did he have to shout at me so loudly? And then it was upon me, that searing pain in my chest, stabbing and growing. I dashed for the kitchen to get a knife to cut it out, but the doorway wasn't there. My guide caught me, held me, and in an hour (or so it seemed), it passed.

"Then, I dreamed that I got into a subway, thinking that I would ride it to the end of the line. At once these words, 'end of the line,' assumed awful and multiple proportions. I felt drawn and impelled towards this 'end of the line' where Some Thing was waiting and beckoning. I felt there I might find fulfillment or destruction, or both.

"At other times, I awakened into an increasingly incredible and terrifying world. I stood on the edge of a giant elevator shaft, which extended down into the infinite. And insane-looking men kept passing into the elevators and coming out again—the same men, over and over

"Then it was pleasant for a while. A ray of sunshine came in the window and illuminated not only the room but the inside of our bodies. I was light, I floated. I could float up into the sky. I went to the window, but it was locked; the door, that was the way to fly! I was out of it before my guide could catch me and flying down the stairs. And then the sickening pain in my left shoulder (I afterwards found that I had been caught at the bottom of the stairs, and that my shoulder had been dislocated at that moment). The pain overwhelmed me, and I could no longer recognize people.

"It was later that I began to have some contact in the drab ward of the hospital, but not for four weeks was I free enough of hallucinations and ordered enough in thought and action to be released. Now, three months later, I am approaching a point at which I can return to college.

"What about consciousness expansion and mystic experience and new meaning to life? A few of my friends insist that they have all these, and perhaps some do. But it is all too easy to term a rapid jumble of thoughts an increase in consciousness if your friend considers that he has had a mystic experience merely because he has for the first time been able to talk with friends about his feelings and theories; what I don't know about him is whether his feelings are the influence of the drug or the influence of the group."*

Counsel and Information

The professional staffs of the Health Services and the Counseling Services at many colleges have made deliberate efforts to study not only the medical-pharmacological facts which are available, but also the psycho-physical and psycho-social dimensions which surround student use. The purpose of these studies has been to help students who express quandaries about their real or potential experimentation in this area. Doctors and counselors, as others, hope that students will avoid the risks involved in the use of any drugs. Usually, the setting of the Health and Counseling Services offers an opportunity for confidential consultation when students become perplexed.

* Many details from both 'trips' were taken from *Varieties of Psychedelic Experience* by R. E. L. Masters and J. Houston.

Conclusions

As a direct result of approaching the drug question unobjectively, many college campuses throughout the nation have been faced with an awkward uproar caused by secrecy and subterfuge, used to discover drug use. The goal in such cases has been essentially to isolate and discipline the drug user with as little notice as possible.

The committee contends that such an approach creates more long-term problems than it solves. We hope that the universities will be able to handle such cases, if they do arise. But at the same time, if the university is to have "jurisdiction" in such cases, it must also have responsibility. The colleges—on whose campuses drug use has spread so rapidly—should take a much more active role in increasing the amount of information available, and when the time comes, of evaluating that information in terms of the legal structures.

The purposes of this publication have been to inform and to express concern and interest in drug use on campuses. The drug question can no longer be avoided; it must be rationally presented and evaluated, if the present problems are to be dealt with.

Bibliography: Psychedelics

Abramson, H. A., editor, The Use of LSD in Psychotherapy and Alcoholism, Bobbs-Merrill, New York, 1967.

Abramson, H. A., editor, The Use of LSD in Psychotherapy, Josiah Macy, Jr. Foundation Publications, New York, 1960.

Barron, F., et al., "The Hallucinogenic Drugs," Scientific American, vol. 210, April 1964, pp. 29-37.

Blum, Richard, editor, Utopiates: The Use and Users of LSD-25, Atherton Press, New York, 1964.

Cohen, S., and Ditman, K. S., "Prolonged Adverse Reactions to Lysergic Acid Diethylamide," Arch. Gen. Psychiatry, vol. 8, 1963, pp. 475-480.

Cohen, S., et al., "Short-Term Effects of LSD on Anxiety, Attitudes and Performance," J. Nerv. Ment. Disorders, vol. 139, no. 3, September 1964.

Cohen, Sidney, The Beyond Within: The LSD Story. Atheneum, New York, 1965.

Harvard Health Services, Harvard Report on Drugs, Cambridge, 1967.

Huxley, Aldous, Island, Bantam Paperback, New York, 1962.

Huxley, Aldous, The Doors of Perception; Heaven and Hell, Penguin Books, London, 1959.

Klüver, Heinrich, Mescal the Divine Plant and the Mechanism of Hallucinogens, University of Chicago Press, Chicago, 1967.

Leary, Timothy, "How to Change Behavior," Clinical Psychology, vol. 4, 1961, pp. 211 ff.

Leary, Timothy, "Playboy Interview," Playboy, August 1966.

Leary, Timothy, et al., The Psychedelic Experience, University Books, New Hyde Park, 1964.

Lindemann, E., and Clarke, L. D., "Modifications in the Ego Structure and Personality Reactions under the Influence of the Effects of Drugs," Amer. J. Psychiatry, vol. 108, 1952, pp. 561-567.

Louria, Donald, Nightmare Drugs, Pocket Books, New York, 1966.

Masters, R. E. L., and Houston, J., Varieties of Psychedelic Experience, Holt, Rinehart, and Winston, New York, 1966.

May, Rollo, editor, Existential Psychology, Random House, New York, 1961.

McGlothlin, W. H., et al. "Short-Term Effects of LSD," J. Nerv. Ment. Disorders, vol. 139, 1964, pp. 266-273.

Mogar, R. E., and Savage, C., "Personality Change Associated with Psychedelic (LSD) Therapy: A Preliminary Report," Psychotherapy, vol. 1, 1964, pp. 154-162.

Mogar, R. E., "Search and Research with Psychedelics," Review of General Semantics, vol. 22, no. 4, December 1965, pp. 393-405.

Osmond, H., and Hoffer, A., The Hallucinogens, Academic Press, New York, 1967.

Psychedelic Review, nos. 1-7, 1963-1965.

Savage, C., et al., "The Effects of Psychedelic Therapy on Values, Personality, and Behavior," Journal of Neuropsychiatry (Belgium), vol. 2, no. 3.

Slotkin, J. S., The Peyote Religion, Free Press of Glencoe, New York, 1956.

Solomon, D., editor, LSD: The Consciousness Expanding Drug, Putnam, New York, 1964.

Solomon, D., editor, The Marijuana Papers, Bobbs-Merrill, Indianapolis, 1966.

Ungerleider, J. T., et al., "Dangers of LSD," Journal of the American Medical Association, August 8, 1966.

White House Conference on Narcotic and Drug Abuse, Government Printing Office, Washington, 1962.

Drug Class	(trade)	Name ("common")	(chemical)	
*Amphetamine	Dexedrine	"dexies"	Dextro-amphetamine	⎫ Stimulants
*Amphetamine	Methedrine	"crystal," "speed"	Methamphetamine	
Amphetamine	Benzedrine	"bennies"	Benzo-amphetamine	⎭
*Barbiturate	Seconal (Fast acting, short lasting—4 hours)	"red devils"	Seco-barbital	⎫
*Barbiturate	Nembutal (Medium acting, medium lasting—6 hours)	"yellow jackets"	Nemo-barbital	
*Barbiturate	Phenobarbital	"phennies"	Pheno-barbital	Sedatives
Barbiturate	Amytal (Slow acting, long lasting—6-8 hours)	"blue heavens"	Amo-barbital	
Barbiturate	Tuinal (Fast acting, long lasting)		50% Seconal, 50% Amytal	⎭
Amphetamine and Barbiturate	Dexamil { Dextro amphetamine / Amo-barbital			⎫ Used medically to suppress appetite and to "stabilize" mood
Amphetamine and Barbiturate	Synitan { Amphetamine-tanate / Seco-barbital			⎭

*Most widely used by students

Copyright © 1968 by Princeton University Student Committee on Mental Health All rights reserved L C Card 68 30831 No part of this book may be reproduced in any form or by any means without written permission from the Princeton University Student Committee on Mental Health, Princeton, New Jersey, 08540

Introduction: Amphetamines / Barbiturates

The use of amphetamines and barbiturates on college campuses is a fairly recent occurrence. While such drugs appear to be used by a relatively small number, their potential danger makes it worthwhile to present information about them. Accordingly the Committee has prepared a brief overview of the subject. The study is not a professional view of the amphetamines and the barbiturates, although professionals were consulted, and although Committee members did research into their particular units. As with our study on the psychedelics, this one is most of all a statement of concern—concern which will, hopefully, lead to more interest and study of the problems on all college campuses.

Legal Aspects

It is beyond the scope of this report to explain the complex of state and federal law. However, some general remarks may be helpful.

The non-prescribed use of amphetamines and barbiturates is illegal. Furthermore, the future problems—in employment and admission to graduate school, for example—of a police record of "drug abuse" are significant.

Briefly, with the exception of marijuana and hashish, New Jersey law classifies the use of amphetamines and barbiturates with the psychedelics. In New Jersey, almost all convicted users of amphetamines, any of its optical isomers, any salt of an amphetamine, any salt of an optical isomer of an amphetamine, or of any barbiturate and any barbiturate salt are by law disorderly persons. Any person who illegally uses or is under the influence of, or who possesses or has under his control, or sells, dispenses, or gives away amphetamines or barbiturates is by law a disorderly person. Also any person who shall obtain, or attempt to obtain possession of the administration of amphetamines or barbiturates by fraud, forgery, concealment of material fact, deceit, misrepresentation, or subterfuge is by law a disorderly person. The penalty for disorderly person offenses is a fine of no more than $1000 and/or a term of imprisonment up to one year.

Any individual adjudged a disorderly person for amphetamine or barbiturate use has the option of being priced upon probation on condition that such individual admit himself to a state or county mental hospital.

Medical Aspects

The effects on the human body and mind of barbiturates and amphetamines are more widely understood than those of the psychedelics. The Committee feels that the use of barbiturates and amphetamines is potentially more deleterious than the use of psychedelics.

Amphetamines

Amphetamines are stimulants. Their use produces a variety of symptoms, not all of which, however, may be experienced by any one user at any particular time. The most common physical responses to these drugs are wakefulness, loss of appetite, a feeling of increased confidence, and sometimes euphoria. A sense of hyper-achievement is sometimes present, but it may be coupled with loss of judgment. To cite an extreme case: A girl who had used dexedrine to stay awake all night so she could study for an examination wrote what she thought was a magnificent essay. In fact, she had written for three hours over and over on the same line.

Psychological response to amphetamine use may include hallucination, confusion, anxiety, paranoid thinking, and delirium, though not all symptoms may be present at one time, nor must they follow that particular order. These changes may make the user assaultive and combative.

Overdosage may produce restlessness, dizziness, irritability and even tremor. Intravenous injections of amphetamines ("shooting," "mainlining") is more likely to result in overdosage than taking them by mouth. In addition, the dirty equipment often used by drug groups may lead to hepatitis. In the extreme, moreover, convulsions, coma, possibly chronic psychosis and eventually death can ensue.

The amphetamines are addicting, although addiction occurs rarely and only with high dosages. Tolerance for the effects of usage is prominent, and increasing doses are necessary to produce the same high at frequent intervals. (See table for the names of the most commonly used amphetamines.)

Barbiturates

Barbiturates are depressants. Some of the physical symptoms of use may include dizziness, loss of judgment and drowsiness. In some cases, moreover, the barbiturates may have a psychological effect and can produce feelings of excitement reminiscent of alcoholic intoxication. When the effects of the drug wear off, hangover is common. In addition one may experience temporary interference (a few hours) with normal behavior, thinking and motor activities. Alcohol consumption reduces tolerance to barbiturates. For this reason, small overdoses of these drugs taken by someone who is intoxicated may often be fatal. Overdoses of barbiturates can produce coma and death. It has been estimated that 3,000 deaths a year are caused by such overdosage.

As with the amphetamines, tolerance for the barbiturates is common, so that increasing doses are necessary to produce the same effect when the drugs are taken frequently over a period of time. Such usage may, in a few individuals, lead to habituation and addiction (physiological dependence). The addiction to barbiturates is more severe for most people than an addiction to heroin. Withdrawal from them is more likely to be fatal. (See table for most commonly used barbiturates.)

Sociological Aspects

Any honest discussion of social use of amphetamines and barbiturates on college campuses must admit before it begins that the conclusions it derives are, at best, general statements based on partial evidence. Sociological information on these drugs is extremely limited, so that the Committee was not able to make any distinctions among the type of users that take each of these drugs. However, some general statements may help to give a broad, if somewhat sketchy, picture of this kind of drug use.

The only drug in this family which appears to be used with any degree of frequency is methedrine. As far as the Committee is aware, there is no ritual for its consumption, as there is with marijuana, and it is usually not taken as a group activity. When methedrine is combined with other drugs, the social aspects of these other drugs may be primary.

A methedrine addict, or "meth head" as he is often called, may when "high" on the drug, move from one social contact to another in rapid and disjointed order, bored and dissatisfied with any one association. He may prefer those who can meet him at his stimulated level to others not using the drug. Because a methedrine user is somewhat incoherent during the latter phases of a high (which may be continued by frequent dosage until he becomes unconscious due either to exhaustion or malnutrition) he is likely to be considered a poor social member of any group and might find himself outside any social group, alone.

The use of other amphetamines is small. In general,

drugs like methedrine have greatest appeal to those members of the "drug culture" who like to experiment.

The social use of barbiturates on college campuses—as far as the Committee is aware—is more limited than that of the amphetamines. In general, those who take barbiturates for kicks tend to become continual and not occasional users. The users, generally, are looking for a different type of "high" than the users of the psychedelics or amphetamines. While the latter produces what may be considered an "upward high" which results in at least greater apparent powers of perceptivity, the former produces a "downward" or oblivion type "high" which tends toward consciousness contraction not expansion. For this reason, barbiturate users usually do not take stimulants or psychedelics.

Since barbiturate use can produce effects similar to alcoholic intoxication, it does not really lend itself to the form of "insight" communal activity such as is found among the users of the psychedelics. The barbiturate user may drop out of society in much the same manner as the alcoholic.

Barbiturates are often mixed with alcohol, amphetamines, and sometimes used with the potent psychedelics, like LSD. When used with alcohol, the barbiturates may produce a high similar to alcoholic intoxication, or if the user is unlucky, the mixture may cause death. Barbiturates are sometimes used alternately with amphetamines. An "up and down" cycle is more or less maintained where the barbiturates counteract the restless insomnia produced by the amphetamines. This kind of "pill orientation," however, may seriously affect the user's judgment of his psychic and physical balance.

There are, however, commercial mixtures of amphetamines and barbiturates which doctors employ to suppress appetite and to "stabilize" mood (see table). Barbiturates (and tranquillizers) sometimes are used to counteract the effects of the potent psychedelics like LSD.

Counsel and Information

Outside of medical use, amphetamines and barbiturates appear to present such risks that the individual would be well advised to avoid the temptation to experiment with these drugs. However, the Counseling Services and the Health Services welcome the opportunity to talk confidentially with students who have further questions concerning this complex area of behavior.

Bibliography: Amphetamines / Barbiturates

Goodman, Louis, et al., The Pharmacological Basis of Therapeutics, Macmillan, New York, 1965.

Kalant, Oriana, The Amphetamines: Toxicity and Addiction, University of Toronto Press, Toronto, Canada, 1966.

GPSR Authorized Representative: Easy Access System Europe - Mustamäe tee 50, 10621 Tallinn, Estonia, gpsr.requests@easproject.com

www.ingramcontent.com/pod-product-compliance
Lightning Source LLC
Chambersburg PA
CBHW071935240426
43668CB00038B/1803